DELAWARE
The First State

TEN TOP FACTS ABOUT DELAWARE

★ ★ ★ ★ ★ ★ ★ ★ ★ ★ ★ ★ ★

State nicknames: The First State, The Diamond State, The Blue Hen State, Small Wonder

State motto: Liberty and Independence

Capital: Dover

Area: 2,489 square miles

State flower: Peach blossom

State tree: American holly

State bird: Blue hen

State insect: Ladybug

State fish: Weakfish

State drink: Milk

Photo credits:

p. 4: Courtesy of The United States Mint; p. 5: (all) The Granger Collection, New York; p. 6: (top) Delaware Tourism Office, (bottom) The Granger Collection; p. 7: (both) Delaware Tourism Office; p. 8: The Granger Collection; p. 9: Library of Congress; p. 10: Delaware Tourism Office; p. 11: (top) "The Underground Railroad" by Charles T. Webber/The Granger Collection, (bottom) Kevin Fleming/Delaware Tourism Office; p. 12: Delaware Tourism Office; p. 13: (top) Delaware Tourism Office, (bottom) Terence Roberts; p. 14: Kevin Fleming/Delaware Tourism Office; p. 15: Delaware Tourism Office; p. 16: (both) Delaware Tourism Office; p. 17: Delaware Tourism Office; p. 18: (both) Delaware Tourism Office; p. 19: (top) Delaware Tourism Office, (bottom) The Granger Collection; p. 20: Kevin Fleming/Delaware Tourism Office, (center) James Watt/Animals Animals, Chatham, NY; p. 22: (top left) The Library Company of Philadelphia, (bottom left) Historical Society of Delaware, (top right) Brown Brothers, Sterling, PA, (bottom right) Historical Society of Delaware; p. 23: Historical Society of Delaware.

All other illustrations by John Speirs.

ISBN 0-439-20677-4

THE
Jim Henson
— COMPANY —

12 11 10 9 8 7 6 5 4 3 2 1   0 1 2 3 4 5/0

Designed by Madalina Stefan

Printed in the U.S.A.

First Scholastic printing, September 2000

DELAWARE
The First State

By Alexandra Hanson-Harding

SCHOLASTIC INC.

New York   Toronto   London   Auckland   Sydney   Mexico City   New Delhi   Hong Kong

A Celebration of the Fifty States

★ ★ ★ ★ ★ ★ ★ ★ ★ ★ ★ ★ ★

In January 1999, the U.S. Mint started an ambitious ten-year program to commemorate each of the fifty United States. Over the next several years (through 2008), they will issue five newly designed quarters each year.

One side (obverse) of each new quarter will display the profile of George Washington and the words Liberty, In God We Trust, *and* United States of America. *The other side (reverse) will feature a design honoring a specific state's unique history, the year it became a state, the year of the quarter's issue, and the words* E Pluribus Unum *(Latin for "from many, one"). The quarters are being issued in the order in which the states joined the union, beginning with the thirteen original colonies.*

To find out more about the 50 State Quarters™ program, visit the official U.S. Mint Web site at www.usmint.gov.

Delaware's Quarter:
The Famous Ride of Caesar Rodney

Before the United States became a nation, Caesar Rodney was one of three delegates chosen to represent Delaware at the Continental Congress in Philadelphia. The Continental Congress was a group of colonial leaders who were opposed to British rule. Tensions between Great Britain and the American Colonies had been growing ever since the colonies were established. In July 1776, the Continental Congress decided to vote on whether or not to declare the colonies' independence. One of Delaware's three representatives was ready to vote yes; another planned to vote no. Without Rodney's "yes" vote, Delaware would not be on record supporting independence.

Rodney was at his plantation in Dover and received word of the vote late on July 1. He galloped off on the eighty-mile journey through a storm-filled night, and arrived during the last minutes of debate, tired and mud-soaked, to cast his vote for independence. On July 4, two days later, the delegates issued the Declaration of Independence. Caesar Rodney's vote had helped to change the course of history.

Rodney served as a general during the Revolutionary War and as Delaware's governor after that. But it is for this heroic ride that he is remembered on the U.S. quarter commemorating Delaware.

A State's Beginnings

Native American longhouses

Long before independence from England was declared, Delaware was settled by two groups of Indians — the Lenni-Lenape to the north and the Nanticoke to the south. They lived in bark longhouses and wigwams alongside rivers.

For many years, the Lenni-Lenape and the Nanticoke traded with the Europeans. Eventually, most of Delaware's Indians would be forced by U.S. soldiers to relocate to Oklahoma.

Native American wigwam

Lapowinsa, a Lenape chief

An early Swedish log cabin in Lewes

In 1631, a group of Dutch explorers tried to settle in what is now Lewes, Delaware — but were driven out by local Indians within a year.

The first permanent settlement in Delaware began in 1638, when two Swedish ships, the *Kalmar Nyckel* and the *Vogel Grip*, landed on the banks of a river (which they named the Christina, after their queen) and started the colony of New Sweden. The first log cabins in America were built here. The settlers traded with Indians for beaver pelts and tobacco. But a fierce competition grew between the people of New Sweden and Dutch traders from farther north. In 1655, the Dutch captured the colony.

New Sweden and the Dutch

Several early European explorers visited Delaware, among them Captain Samuel Argall from the colony of Virginia, who sailed up the river into the bay that borders the state. He named the river after Thomas West, Lord De La Warr (or Delaware), the first governor of Virginia. Later the state took its name from the river.

Trading in early Delaware

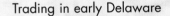

The Duke of York gives the land of Delaware to William Penn

Old State House, Dover

In 1664, the Dutch colony was captured by the English. In 1682, England's Duke of York gave the land that is now Delaware to William Penn, the leader of the new colony of Pennsylvania. The Three Lower Counties, as the area was called, remained tied to Pennsylvania until the Revolutionary War. William Penn allowed the counties to have their own legislature but they shared the same governor (Penn himself was the first governor).

Finally, in 1776, the Three Lower Counties' leaders held a convention and declared themselves "the Delaware State." It was a good time to declare independence — the Revolutionary War was about to begin.

The three dates represent the years changes were made to the Great Seal of the state of Delaware.

GREAT SEAL OF THE STATE OF DELAWARE

LIBERTY AND INDEPENDENCE

1793·1847·1907

Revolution

After Caesar Rodney's stormy ride, Delaware soldiers fought bravely in many battles throughout the war, but only one battle was actually fought in the state — at Cooch's Bridge near the city of Newark, in September 1777. The Stars and Stripes are believed to have first been shown at this battle.

In spite of their small army, the Delaware soldiers did make a name for themselves; they became known as the Blue Hen's Chickens.

During the Revolutionary War, Delaware raised an army of four thousand men. Some men in Captain John Caldwell's company brought blue hen chickens (a type of chicken with bluish feathers) with them. The soldiers used them to stage cockfights to amuse themselves during quiet times. The soldiers became famous for these fighting chickens and began to run into battle yelling, "We're sons of the blue hen and we're game to the end." Later, all Delaware soldiers were called the Blue Hen's Chickens. Today the blue hen is Delaware's official state bird.

These soldiers joined Washington's army again at the Battle of Brandywine, one of the largest battles of the Revolutionary War, just north of the Delaware border in Pennsylvania.

Blue Hen's Chicken

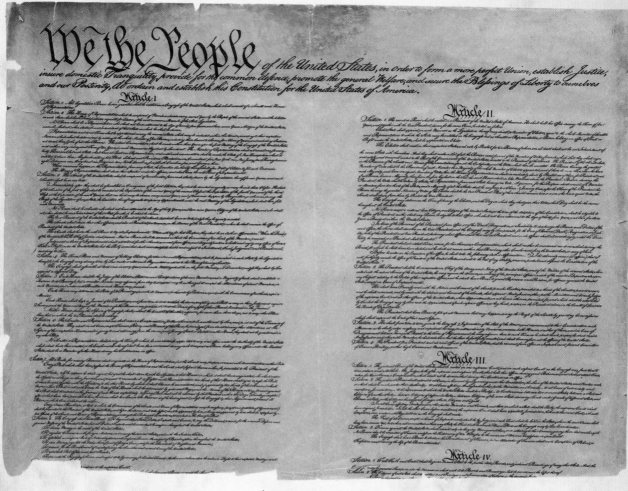

The U.S. Constitution

In September 1783, the United States won independence from British rule, and a few years later, in December 1787, Delaware became the first state to ratify, or agree to, the U.S. Constitution. That is why Delaware is known as the First State.

From Flour Mills to Gunpowder Mills

In 1785, Delaware inventor Oliver Evans created a new kind of flour-milling machinery that revolutionized the flour business. By 1790, mills along the Brandywine River in Wilmington were shipping 300,000 bushels of flour a year. At one time, more than one hundred mills of various types lined the river. In 1802, the most important of these factories opened when a French immigrant named E. I. du Pont started a gunpowder mill on the banks of the river.

A few years later, another war sprang up between the British and the Americans. During this conflict, the War of 1812, the British blockaded the Delaware River. The British demanded supplies from the town of Lewes (pronounced Lewis), but the townspeople refused to turn them over. An American colonel, Samuel B. Davis, had only about fifty men, but he marched them in and out of Lewes so many times that the British thought they were facing a large army. When British ships bombarded Lewes, civilians crept through tall grass, picked up the British cannonballs, and gave them to American soldiers to shoot them back. In fact, the British were so off-target with their bombardment that the Americans made up a rhyme about them:

*"The commander and all his men
Shot a dog and killed a hen."*

After a while, the British gave up and Delaware was saved. Meanwhile, the DuPont Company began to grow rich through its sales of gunpowder.

Eleutherian Mills,
E.I. du Pont's house in Wilmington

"The Underground Railroad"

The Struggle over Slavery

Slavery was legal in Delaware, though it was frowned upon in some parts of the state and many of its black people were free. Many Delawareans, white and black, worked to help slaves escape through the Underground Railroad, a secret system established to help move fugitive slaves to Canada or other safe places in the North.

During the Civil War, Delaware lawmakers decided the state would remain part of the Union. Out of the state's small population of 112,000 people, more than 13,000 young men went to fight for the North. A few hundred went to fight for the South. No major battles took place in Delaware, but its soldiers fought bravely in other battles. The DuPont mill was busy again during this war — as much as half

the gunpowder used by the North was made by DuPont. More than 12,500 Confederate prisoners were housed at Fort Delaware, a five-sided fortress on Pea Patch Island in Delaware Bay. Visitors can still see the fortress today.

Fort Delaware, Pea Patch Island

Delaware Today

In the 1980s, the Financial Center Development Act gave businesses many tax advantages if they moved or brought money into the state. This act brought so many banks and other businesses to Delaware that more than half of the companies on *Fortune* magazine's Top 500 list are incorporated here. Many people still farm in Delaware, but the state's largest employer is DuPont. Delaware is sometimes called the Corporate Capital of the World.

This tiny state on the eastern seaboard of the United States is bordered by the Atlantic Ocean and the Delaware River. It also shares borders with the states of New Jersey, Pennsylvania, and Maryland. Situated on the Delmarva Peninsula (named for **Del**aware, **Mar**yland, and **V**irgini**a**), Delaware has only three counties — New Castle, Kent, and Sussex — the smallest number of any state. It is the second smallest state in the country, only half the size of Los Angeles County, California! Its greatest distance north to south is ninety-six miles; east to west, thirty-five miles. At some points, Delaware is only eight miles wide! The only states with smaller populations are Alaska, Nevada, and Wyoming.

Downtown Wilmington

Thomas Jefferson once called Delaware the Diamond State because its location — and its loyalty to the Revolutionary cause — made it so valuable. It is located between the north and south, has access to the ocean and to the Delaware River, and is near major cities like Philadelphia, Washington, D.C., Baltimore, and New York.

State flag of Delaware

The Delaware Memorial Bridge spans the Delaware River and connects Delaware to New Jersey. Traffic was so heavy after the bridge was built in 1951 that a second, twin span was opened in 1968.

13

Things to Do and Places to See

Rehoboth Beach

This town along the Atlantic Ocean is known as the Nation's Summer Capital because so many people head there from Washington, D.C., each summer. There's a lot to do, from hanging out on the milelong boardwalk to playing in arcades or racing go-carts. But the main attraction is the warm blue water and sparkly sand. In fact, Delaware has twenty-five miles of ocean coastline, which includes several other well-known resort towns, like Bethany Beach and Fenwick Island. They are great places for swimming, wind surfing, or fishing.

Every August, more than one hundred teams compete to build the most elaborate sand sculptures at the Rehoboth Beach Sand Castle Contest.

Bicycle Route One

Delaware has great biking because most of it is level, and it has lots of small towns, farms, and ocean views to enjoy. The state even has a border-to-border, marked bike route called Bicycle Route One. The route stretches 147 miles from Brandywine Creek State Park in the north to Fenwick Island State Park along the coast in the south.

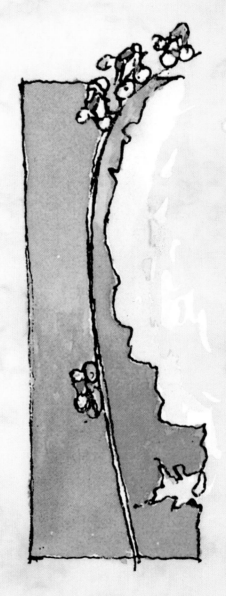

Dover Downs

One of the hottest sporting events in Delaware is NASCAR's "Monster Mile," which draws more than 100,000 racing fans to Dover Downs International Speedway each spring and fall.

Wilmington

Wilmington is the largest — and oldest — city in Delaware. You can visit Fort Christina State Park where the Swedes first landed; often a replica of the *Kalmar Nyckel,* the Swedish tall ship that brought the first settlers to Delaware, is docked there. You can visit Old Swedes Church, which was built in 1698 and is the oldest Protestant church still in use in the United States. Its pipe organ has 913 pipes! The city also has many museums, parks, and historical buildings.

Kalmar Nyckel

Dutch House Museum

The Old Swedes Church

Brandywine Valley

One of the most popular museums in the historic Brandywine Valley is the Hagley Museum, where E. I. du Pont first started making gunpowder nearly two hundred years ago. You can see how a water-powered gunpowder factory worked and learn about the life of its workers.

There are also other museums, like Winterthur — famous for its collection of early American furniture — the Delaware History Museum, and the Delaware Art Museum.

Winterthur Museum

Dover

Dover is the state's capital, and it was here the state was born. The Old State House, built in 1792, is one of the oldest in the United States. Dover is also home to the Dover Air Force Base, where the nation's largest cargo planes are stored, and sometimes are available to the public for viewing. Some are so huge that they can carry one hundred cars at a time! Those who really like planes can also go to the Air Mobility Command Museum, located in an old-fashioned World War II hangar, and check out cool antique planes used in World War II, Vietnam, and other conflicts. History lovers can visit the John Dickinson Plantation, the home of an early governor of Delaware.

Dover Air Force Base

New Castle

Lewes

Lewes is a little seaside town with a long history. Dutch settlers first came here in 1631. Later, pirates such as Captain Kidd prowled off the shore of Lewes. It is said there are chests of buried treasure near the town. Because there is so much shipping in the area, the Coast Guard station is one of the busiest and most important in the United States. Lewes has a small historical village where visitors can see what life was like there in the eighteenth and nineteenth centuries. If you like boat rides, you can take the ferry between Lewes and the Victorian town of Cape May, New Jersey.

Captain Kidd

New Castle

The colonial town of New Castle was established in the 1600s and was once the capital of Delaware. Today it looks almost the same as it did hundreds of years ago. With its cobblestone streets, old brick sidewalks, and quaint houses, you almost expect to see George Washington walking down the street!

Among its famous buildings are the old Court House (Delaware's colonial capitol), the old Dutch House (the oldest dwelling in the state, built around 1651 and filled with objects from colonial times), and the Amstel House (the former home of one of Delaware's governors).

19

The Atlantic flyway

Bombay Hook National Wildlife Refuge

During migration seasons, Bombay Hook has the greatest concentration of snow geese in North America (more than 130,000!) on its 15,000 acres of marshes, woods, and ponds. In fact, Delaware is the major staging area for eighty percent of the snow geese in the Atlantic flyway. More than two hundred other species, including bald eagles, also visit the refuge each year. There are three observation towers and plenty of hiking trails for those who love to see nature in the wild.

Chesapeake and Delaware Wildlife Area

Building of the Delaware and Chesapeake Canal started in 1804. This canal created a shortcut between the Delaware River and the Chesapeake Bay and reduced ships' journeys by hundreds of miles. When it was finished in 1829, it allowed goods to be carried to Philadelphia quickly. Now it is flanked by a lovely park with twelve miles of trails for biking, hiking, and horseback riding. The canal is part of the intercoastal waterway.

Cape Henlopen

Cape Henlopen, located near Lewes, is an important breeding area for an endangered seabird called the piping plover. Whales and dolphins appear off the coast of Cape Henlopen and boats take visitors on whale-watching trips in this area. Fishing is popular, too. Cape Henlopen has the tallest sand dune (eighty feet!) between Cape Hatteras, North Carolina, and Cape Cod, Massachusetts. The Great Delaware Kite Festival takes place on the beach in Cape Henlopen Park.

The Great Delaware Kite Festival

Humpback whale

Save the Horseshoe Crabs!

Delaware Bay has the largest population of horseshoe crabs in the world, and people have harvested them for years. But now environmentalists are worried because so many are being harvested. The loss of too many of these creatures will threaten another form of wildlife that depends on them — birds.

One and a half million birds migrate north along the Atlantic flyway each spring. Horseshoe crab eggs are an important source of food for them. Now Delaware is pushing to restrict collection of these sea creatures.

Famous People from Delaware

Richard Allen (1760–1831)

Richard Allen was born a slave, but that didn't stop him from following his religious calling. He started his preaching career on the plantation where he was enslaved — and soon converted his master. He was ordained as a minister in 1799. He and his brother worked hard to save money to buy their freedom. In 1816, he helped to found the African Methodist Episcopal denomination and became its first bishop. Allen also operated a station on the Underground Railroad.

Annie Jump Cannon (1863–1941)

Annie Jump Cannon, born in Dover, reached for the stars and became one of America's best-known astronomers. She is credited with discovering three hundred stars and other heavenly objects. Her tremendous scientific work, the *Henry Draper Catalog of Stellar Spectra,* was one of the most extensive scholarly publications ever attempted. She is remembered as the "census taker of the sky."

Eleuthère Irénée du Pont (1771–1834)

In 1804, Eleuthère Irénée du Pont spent $36,000 to bring supplies and equipment across the ocean all the way from France. He then set up a gunpowder factory on the banks of the Brandywine River. He had studied chemistry in France with a brilliant scientist named Antoine Lavoisier. With his scientific knowledge and experience he was able to make a superior product and his factory quickly became successful. DuPont gunpowder was used to fend off the British during the War of 1812 and later was used during the Civil War. Under his heirs, the company branched out and grew to become the richest chemical company in the world.

Thomas Garrett (1789–1871)

Pennsylvania-born Thomas Garrett, a Quaker, lived in Wilmington, and was one of the most famous "stationmasters" on the Underground Railroad. He worked with Harriet Tubman, another famous abolitionist, to free more than 2,500 slaves. Today a plaque at Fourth and Shipley Streets marks the site where his house once stood, and a park in Wilmington— the Garrett-Tubman Riverfront Park—is named for the two friends who helped bring an end to slavery.

Howard Pyle (1853—1911)

Born in Wilmington, Howard Pyle was one of the most famous illustrators of his day. The bold lines and colors used in his illustrations for classic children's books, along with his extensive research into his subjects, made his drawings stand out. Some of his favorite subjects included medieval history, U.S. history, and pirates.

Today, the Delaware Art Museum in Wilmington has the world's largest collection of Pyle's paintings — as well as many paintings by artists he inspired.

Mary Ann Shadd Cary (1823—1893)

Born near Wilmington, Mary Ann Shadd Cary was the oldest of thirteen children in a family of free blacks. Her family's shoemaking shop was a stop on the Underground Railroad. Educated by Quakers, she began to organize a school for African-American children when she was only sixteen. After many years of teaching, Shadd Cary moved to Canada, where she taught freed slaves. In 1869, she became the first woman to enter Howard University's law school—and the first African-American woman to earn a law degree.

Other Famous Delawareans

Joseph Biden, Jr. (1942–   )
A Democratic member of the United States Senate from Delaware since 1973, Joseph Biden gained national attention as a presidential candidate in 1987. The senator grew up in New Castle County, and attended the University of Delaware and Syracuse University College of Law. He is a leader on anticrime and drug policy and is one of the Senate's leading foreign policy experts.

John Dickinson (1732–1808)
This lawyer wrote so many papers against English control of the colonies that he was called the "Penman of the Revolution." Later he became governor of Delaware—and then Pennsylvania.

Henry J. Heimlich (1920–   )
Born in Wilmington, this U.S. surgeon, author, and teacher is known the world over for his development of the lifesaving technique for choking victims, the Heimlich maneuver.

Randy White (1953–   )
This defensive tackle for the Dallas Cowboys (1975–1988) went to nine Pro Bowls in the 1970s and 1980s, and made it into the Pro Football Hall of Fame.

A Rare Kind of Courage

By 1804, slavery was illegal in all the states north of the Mason-Dixon line (states north of Maryland's border with Pennsylvania). There was a law, however, called the Fugitive Slave Law of 1793, which made it a federal crime to protect a fugitive (runaway) slave in any state. In the two decades before the Civil War, there was increasing pressure to enforce this law, making Canada, where slavery was abolished in 1833, the safest destination for fugitives. A secret system called the Underground Railroad developed to help slaves travel safely to the North; "conductors" would lead the slaves out of the South, then the "stationmasters" would hide the slaves until it was safe for them to continue moving north. Slavery was legal in Delaware but some people, especially many who belonged to the Quaker religion, were against it. One of the most famous of these "stationmasters" was Thomas Garrett. His home in Wilmington was the last stop on the railroad before fugitives crossed into Pennsylvania. The following story is fiction, but Thomas Garrett was real—he helped free 2,500 slaves during his lifetime.

Listen, child, sit yourself down while I tell you the story of a man I once knew, a man named Thomas Garrett. He was a stationmaster on the Underground Railroad. And he was a good friend to a lot of black people who just wanted a chance for freedom.

Back in 1847, I was a slave in Maryland. Those were mean times back then. Once I got whipped for taking a lump of sugar. I worked in the house, taking care of the mistress. She liked the way I fixed her hair and took care of all of her things. One day I was brushing her hair and it tangled, and she slapped me, hard. She said in the most spiteful voice,

"You hurt me on purpose, Araminta, didn't you? Makes me almost glad we're selling you. One day's work on a cotton plantation will make you regret this."

When I heard those words, I was chilled to the bone. As bad as being a slave up in Maryland was, being a slave on a big cotton planta-tion was worse. The work was hot and brutal. And there was almost no way to escape from there. I resolved to make a break for freedom as soon as I could.

Just about that time, an old lady came among us. She said she was a seamstress and had papers to show she was a free black, which some

were. Soon I found out that she wasn't old at all. She was wearing a disguise because she was so well-known as a conductor on the Underground Railroad that every-one knew her face. Her name was Harriet Tubman, and she made her life's work rescuing slaves from the South.

One night, she left for the North under cover of darkness and I went with her, along with six men. It was scary going. We had to wade in brooks so dogs wouldn't follow our scent. We got soaked cross-ing the Choptank River into Delaware. One man wanted to turn back but she put a gun to his head and made him go on.

She knew just where to go, where to find the "stations" on the Underground Railroad. We stopped at different stations all through Delaware, each one about ten to thirty miles apart. We would sneak out at night to go to the next one.

I got sick from all that walking in the water. I began to think I wouldn't make it, and I got a bad fever. Then we ended up at the house of Thomas Garrett, the last station in Delaware. He and she half carried me into the secret part of the house away from prying eyes.

"We must take care of thy friend, Harriet," he said. "She is ill."

Even with the chills, I could tell from all his "thee" and "thy" talk that he was a Quaker, and I was glad. I had heard the Quakers were good to black people and wanted to help them.

He quickly got me tucked into bed. I don't know what happened in the next few days, but when I woke up, Master Garrett brought in a bowl of soup for me to eat and fed it to me gently. He asked me questions about myself.

I asked him why he was so kind to me, since I was only a slave.

He told me that when he was a young man, he saw slavers capture a young, free black woman who worked for his family. He said he had to chase them halfway across the state before he could free her from their clutches. "From that time on," he said, "I have vowed to fight against the evil of slavery."

And then he told me something else—he told me that it was an honor to help people like me. "Thou has a rare kind of courage to run away, Araminta," he said.

A rare kind of courage. I liked that.

Soon, it was time to go. He found a new dress for me, and some shoes. He hired a carriage to take us to freedom in Philadelphia, which was in Pennsylvania—a free state. You can't imagine what it felt like for me to be free—like a stone was taken off my chest. For the first time, I didn't belong to anyone else. I belonged to myself! But we were still in danger. There was a bad law called the Fugitive Slave Law of 1793 that said that any runaway slave could be returned to slavery—and that people in the North would be breaking the law if they protected slaves. Harriet Tubman helped us get all the way to Canada, where we would be safe for sure.

From time to time, she would come up and bring more slaves, and each time she would stop and tell us about her life. I often inquired about Thomas Garrett. One time I asked, she told me he was finally caught and was fined. The fine was harsh—he lost his entire business and everything he owned. The judge who fined him said, "Well, Thomas, I hope never to see you here again."

And Thomas Garrett said, "[Although] thou has left me without a dollar . . . I say to thee and to all in this courtroom, that if anyone knows a fugitive who wants shelter . . . send him to Thomas Garrett and he will befriend him."

And the thing is, he meant it! Soon his friends helped him to restart his business. He kept on helping people. In fact, he never stopped. He had to build an extra room in the back of his house to hide even more slaves.

In 1865, the Civil War finally ended and the Thirteenth Amendment to the Constitution was ratified, putting an end to the cruel practice of slavery. I was able to move back to Delaware. Nobody forgot what our good friend Mr. Garrett had done.

Well, child, I'm old now, but I'll never forget that time of my life. I don't know how I got the strength to flee. But I am glad that there were good people to help me along the way, people like Mr. Thomas Garrett. I want you to remember his name.

Chick-a-licious! A Recipe from Delaware

Back in 1923, a Delaware farmer named Cecile Steele decided to market young broiler chickens. From her first year, when she brought five hundred chickens to market, Delaware has grown to be the seventh largest broiler-chicken-producing state in the United States. Every three years, Sussex County hosts the Delmarva Chicken Festival. It features one of the world's largest frying pans — it's ten feet across and can hold eight hundred chicken quarters at a time!

Here is a recipe from the Delmarva Poultry Industry, Inc., host of the festival. Remember to get an adult to help you!

★ Chili Chicken Nuggets ★

4 boneless, skinless chicken breasts
2 tablespoons butter or margarine, melted
1 tablespoon lime juice
1/2 teaspoon bottled red pepper sauce

3/4 cup cornmeal
1 1/2 teaspoons chili powder
1/2 teaspoon garlic salt
Bottled red salsa

Preheat the oven to 400°F. Cut the chicken into nugget-sized pieces. In a shallow dish, mix together butter or margarine, lime juice, and red pepper sauce. Add the chicken nuggets, stirring to coat on all sides. In a plastic bag, mix together the cornmeal, chili powder, and garlic salt. Add the chicken, several pieces at a time, shaking to coat after each addition. Place the chicken in a single layer on a foil-lined baking sheet. Bake for 15 to 20 minutes or until chicken is brown and fork tender. Serve with salsa for dipping. Makes about 24 nuggets.